The abilities in me

This book is dedicated to the Walker-Parker family

Copyright © 2020 Gemma Keir

All rights reserved. The moral right of the author and illustrator have been asserted. No part of this book may be reproduced, transmitted or stored in any information retrieval system in any form or by any means, graphic, electronic, or mechanical, including photocopying, taping and recording, without prior permission from the copyright owner.

Published by The Abilities In Me
Written by Gemma Keir
Illustrations copyright © 2020 by Adam Walker-Parker
Edited by Emma Lusty and Claire Bunyan

ISBN Paperback: 9781784566951
ISBN Hardback: 9781784566968
First printed in the United Kingdom, 2019

www.theabilitiesinme.com

The abilities in me

Autism

Written by Gemma Keir
Illustrated by Adam Walker-Parker

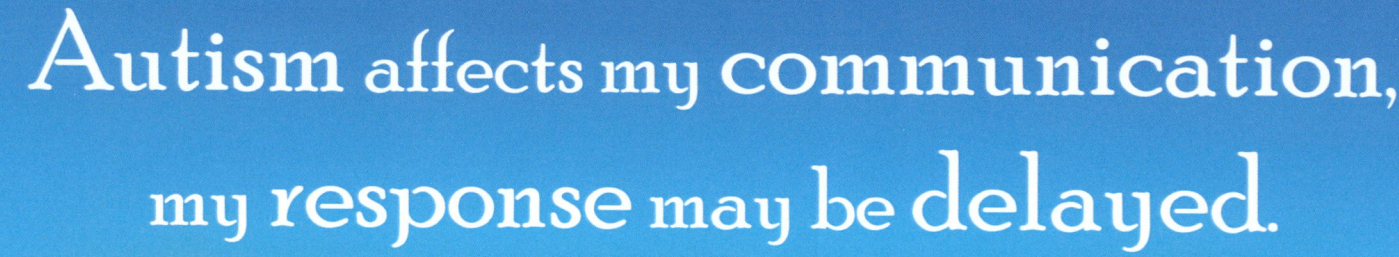
Autism affects my communication, my response may be delayed.

I may just need my ear defenders or space away from the crowd.

A night at home with my family, watching movies on TV.

Write down your super abilities:

What is Autism?

ASD – Autistic Spectrum Disorder

Autism is a lifelong neurological condition which affects how a person communicates and interacts with other people.

It can also affect how they experience, process and interpret the world around them. Autism is referred to as a Spectrum Condition, as each child with a diagnosis of autism will have differing needs and abilities.

Often, autistic people will say that they feel overwhelmed with sights, sounds, smells, information
and feelings, which can make them feel anxious and confused. They may find comfort in repetitive activities, routines and structure to try and make the world a more predictable place. Someone on the Autistic Spectrum may struggle to understand and follow the complexities of social interactions, subtle or abstract meanings, facial expressions and body language. However, in some areas they may have a huge depth of knowledge, skill and expertise, finding ease in situations others may find daunting.

Although autism can bring many challenges to the person themselves and their families it can also bring many positives too. An autistic person is not ill or broken but has a unique, wonderful and equally valuable view of the world.

Information provided by SPACE Hertfordshire charity
Registered charity number - 1172178

SPACE is a Hertfordshire based charity supporting Families with children and young people on the Autistic Spectrum and/or Attention Deficit Hyperactivity Disorder (ADHD) and related conditions. The SPACE Team are predominantly parent carers themselves which gives us a valuable insight into raising children that have additional needs. We support our families in many different ways: We offer numerous monthly support groups running in various locations in Hertfordshire.
Creating a friendly and informal way of meeting other parent/carers in a relaxed, safe environment.

These groups are also attended and supported by many professionals giving families an opportunity to find out about services and how to access them.
We run several low cost or free workshops, conferences and training opportunities throughout the year.
We run extensive exclusive events for parent/carers, families and individuals ranging from Lego clubs, ice skating, outdoor activities, driving, cooking, indoor play, trampoline parks, mindfulness, football and karate to name just a few.

www.spaceherts.org.uk
spaceherts@gmail.com

 /spacehertfordshire

About the Author

My name is Gemma Keir, I am the book author for "The abilities in me" children's book series from Hertfordshire, England. I am a mum to a child with a range of medical conditions, including 22q Deletion who has inspired me to write these incredible stories. I am proud to have received qualifications in Special Educational Needs and Disabilities and Sensory Awareness plus specialist training in Behaviour and Safeguarding. These books provide awareness of a range of needs in children today and will be extremely popular for school settings and families who have a child with these conditions. I aim to change the whole perception of these children by promoting the abilities they do have and prevent potential bullying later in that child's life. I feel that this is possible, because children around them will be taught, from a young age and in a positive light, to have awareness and be open-minded. My vision is for children with special educational needs and disabilities to have a book to read about a character who is just like them. I aim to bring inclusivity to children's literature, acceptance and positivity.

www.theabilitiesinme.com

www.facebook.com/theabilitiesinmebookseries

About the Illustrator

My name is Adam Walker-Parker, I am a professional illustrator from Scotland.
I have worked in the art industry for 12 years now, I began my career as an artist, choosing to paint figurative and wildlife paintings.
I now illustrate children's books and find joy in creating something magical and inspiring for children to see.

www.awalkerparker.com

www.facebook.com/awalkerparkerillustration

www.instagram.com/awalkerparkerillustration

MORE BOOKS COMING SOON

We create children's picture books, based on characters of young children with varying disabilities. Each book will feature a child with a condition, and we aim to create a bright, colourful and positive outlook on every child with special needs. We are all unique and beautiful in every way, shape and form. This collection of books will show how each child can celebrate their abilities within their disability, find acceptance and create awareness to those around them. These books will touch the hearts of your homes, schools and hospital settings, and most importantly, your child will have a book to read, based on a special character, just like them.

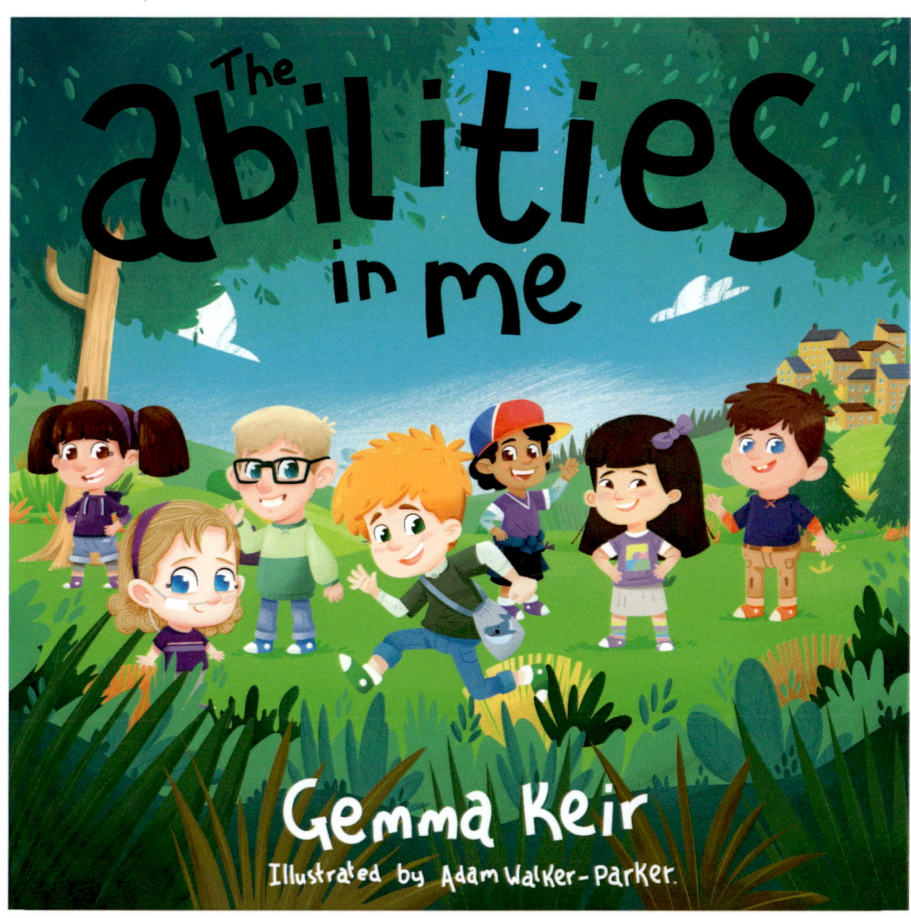

Title: The Abilities In Me - Children's Book Series
Written by Gemma Keir
Cover and Illustrations by Adam Walker-Parker

The abilities in me